The Adventures of Scuba Jack
Copyright 2021 by Beth Costanzo
All rights reserved

Gorillas are the largest apes in the world! Gorillas are found in Central Africa. There are two main species of gorilla, the Eastern Gorilla and the Western Gorilla. The **Western Gorilla** lives in Western Africa and the **Eastern Gorilla** lives in Eastern Africa. Gorillas are mostly herbivores and like to eat roots, shoots, fruit, bark, and wild celery. Sometimes they will eat insects, especially ants! A full grown adult male will eat around 50 pounds of food a day! The males are often twice as big as the females. The males grow to around 5 ½ feet tall and weigh 400 pounds and the females grow to around 4 ½ feet tall and weigh 200 pounds.

A group of gorillas is called a *troop*. A troop is led by a male "silverback" who decides where the troop eats and sleeps. Gorillas climb trees but prefer to spend most of their time on the ground. At night, gorillas will sleep in nests in trees and on the ground. These nests are made of leaves and branches. Baby gorillas will stay in their mother's nests until they are around 2 ½ years old.

Gorillas have hands and feet like humans including opposable thumbs and big toes. But, they are built quite differently than humans which makes them better climbers and better adapted to walking on all fours. Gorillas have long arms that are longer than their legs! They use their long arms to "knuckle walk," which means they use their knuckles on their hands to walk on all fours. It's hard to measure how strong a gorilla really is, but estimates range from around 4 times to 10 times stronger than your average human.

GORILLA ACTIVITIES

www.adventuresofscubajack.com

Tracing Practice

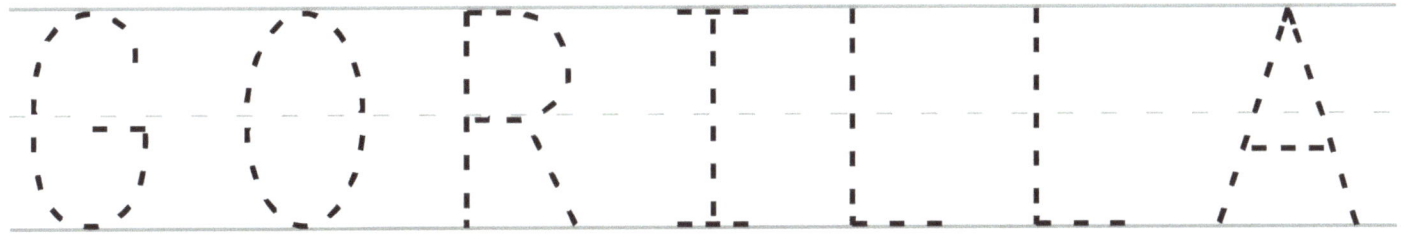

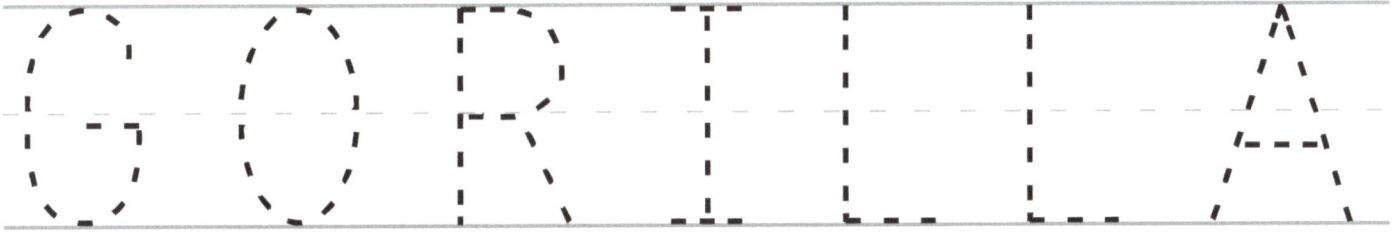

WWW.ADVENTURESOFSCUBAJACK.COM

COUTING PRATICE

1   3   5   2

2   5   1   3

1   3   4   2

1   3   5   2

WWW. ADVENTURESOFSCUBAJACK.COM

GORILLA MAZE

www.adventuresofscubajack.com

COLORING PAGE

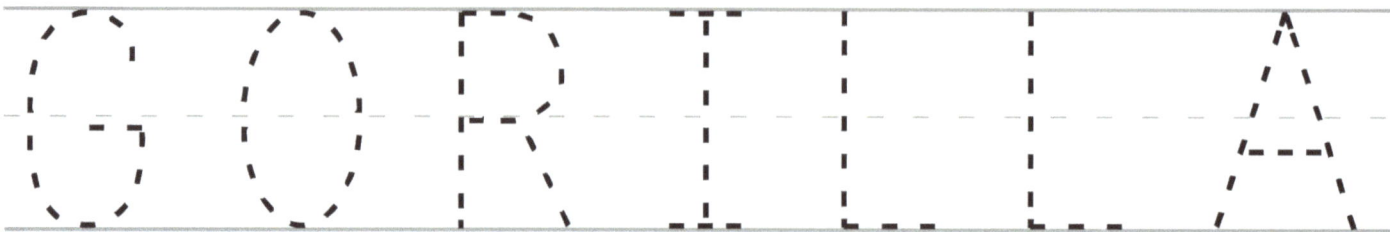

www.adventuresofscubajack.com

CRAFT

WWW.ADVENTURESOFSCUBAJACK.COM

Cut and paste the monsters from short to tall

www.adventuresofscubajack.com

COUNTING

Count the gorillas then circle the correct answer

| 7 9 8 | 10 9 11 |
| 10 8 9 | 11 12 10 |

www.adventuresofscubajack.com

DOT TO DOT

link the dots then color the final image

www.adventuresofscubajack.com

GORILLA CRAFT

Cut the gorilla's parts then glue them together. Then Color your Gorilla!

www.adventuresofscubajack.com

Visit us at:
www.adventuresofscubajack.com

www.ingramcontent.com/pod-product-compliance
Lightning Source LLC
Chambersburg PA
CBHW041439010526
44118CB00002B/127